ANGEL

Ruth Padel researched Greek tragedy, religion and psychology in Oxford, Paris, Berlin and Athens, teaching in London, Crete, and on the sponge-divers' island of Kalymnos. She now lives in London, finishing a book on madness, *Whom Gods Destroy*, to follow *In and out of the Mind* (Princeton University Press, 1992). Her scholarly work, 'exquisitely written word-painting' on madness and self in ancient Greece, has been prized for the 'gruesome brilliance and richness' with which she portrays 'an intense and exotic mental world' (*New York Review of Books*). *Angel*, plunging into psychologically estranged worlds, does something similar. Here too she excels in 'making foreign patterns of thought compellingly vivid' (*Times Literary Supplement*).

Her first collection, *Summer Snow*, was published by Hutchinson in 1990. Her poems have been published widely in Britain and America. She was a prizewinner in the National Poetry Competition in 1992. *Angel* (Bloodaxe Books, 1993) is her second book of poems.

Angel

RUTH PADEL

BLOODAXE BOOKS

ISBN: 1 85224 278 7

First published 1993 by
Bloodaxe Books Ltd,
P.O. Box 1SN,
Newcastle upon Tyne NE99 1SN.

Bloodaxe Books Ltd acknowledges
the financial assistance of Northern Arts.

Cover printing by J. Thomson Colour Printers Ltd, Glasgow.

Printed in Great Britain by
Cromwell Press Ltd, Broughton Gifford, Melksham, Wiltshire.

For Michael Black

Acknowledgements

Acknowledgements are due to the editors of the following publications in which some of these poems, in some version, first appeared: *Acumen, Cambridge Review, Critical Quarterly, European Judaism, Greek Gifts* (Poetry Business Competition 1991), *London Review of Books, The New Yorker, The Observer, Oxford Magazine, Poetry* (Chicago), *Poetry London Newsletter, Poetry Review, The Sunday Times, The Times, The Times Literary Supplement, Verse* and *Writing Women*.

'Trial' was a runner-up in the 1992 National Poetry Competition. 'Indian Red' and 'House of Night' were Commended in the 1991 Poetry Business Competition. 'Angel', and 'Seven with a Cross', are dedicated to Matthew Sweeney.

The author thanks the Royal Literary Fund for generous help; and the Wingate Scholarships for support on other projects while this book was in preparation. Also Jane Davies, very much: for the Toshiba.

Contents

I

Angel

No one sees me. Fathoms up
a nest of rays, all protein,
grey velvet triangles

six metres wing to wing,
a coat on them like a Vymerana,
ripples at the edges, slow,

the way the skite-tooth grass
trembled in lunar winds back home.
So no one knows

and if they read the impress
where my egg sacs
crumbled into bed, work done,

there's nothing they could do.
I listen to the humming
and I wait. Suppose they clawed

one ring from my antenna-bone
up through that tunnel of sea-cow
and acetta-swabs

changing sex halfway through life,
pink to meridian blue,
they'd re-do Linnaeus,

any story of black holes,
re-assign prizes
for the signature of matter,

but still they wouldn't
see what's coming.
How do I know all this?

Baby, where I come from,
we had pre-rusted pictoscopes
to tell us about aliens like you.

The Starling

They are talking of trepanning the Indian starling
because the starling thinks she is the Empress of Oslo
and besides, she is very lonely. The Kissagram boy,
off duty, brought her in from the westwoods
under the flyover, her tertiaries dipped in ink:
smaragdine plus a lavender-cum-royal blue.

She looked, then, a bedraggled poisonous orchid.
We bled her at the hip or wherever roughly
you might expect a hip in all that tininess.
She lies alone on puffed flannel and can't sleep.
I've slipped out, nights, against orders
to feed her cinnamon toast, read her *The Golden Bough*.

Her eye is cloudy, suspicious. She voids phlegm
and half-dreams of a childless woman
killed in a bar in backstreet Friedenstadt,
and that nobody, nobody mourned her
as the starling thinks *she* should be mourned.
Bedlem's Managing Director, the one man

who can save our starling, has evaded diagnosis.
He says she was a present from the King.
After the first incision, he kept his scalpel
under the lid of its Royal Society box
in a self-shaped baize hollow like the bed
of a chestnut in its shell. Or a sharp empty egg.

Trepanning, bloodletting: early seventeenth-century cures for insanity.

12

Trial

I was with Special Force, blue-X-ing raids
to OK surfing on the Colonel's birthday.
Operation Ariel: we sprayed Jimi Hendrix
loud from helis to frighten the slopes
before 'palming. A turkey shoot.

The Nang fogged up. The men you need
are moral and kill like angels. Passionless.
No judgement. Judgement defeats us.
You're choosing between nightmares all the time.
My first tour, we hissed into an encampment
early afternoon, round two. The new directive,

polio. Inoculating kids. It took a while.
As we left, this old man came up, pulled on our
back-lag jeep-hood, yacking. We went back.
They'd come behind us, hacked off
all the inoculated arms. There they were
in a pile, a pile of little arms.

Soon after, all us new recruits turned on
to angel-dust like the rest.
You get it subsidised out there.
The snail can't crawl on the straight
razor and live. I'm innocent.

Foxgloves

I found her recipe
in the *Taunton Evening News*,
reading it out Friday night
as I always did. He made do
in the ioniser room six days
with pinpricks on parchment.

'Two to four cups spring water.
Or use distilled. One heaped tsp. ginseng.
Two tbs. sea-salt crystals. One head
of coltsfoot. One pinch she-wolf's hair
from a *live and shedding wolf.*

This is important. Ask keepers
at your local Wildlife Centre. One ounce
graveyard topsoil from the bed
of someone you revered for courage.
Don't use a shovel. Always replace

any sod you pull up.' When we met
it was September. Spores were out.
Asthma bad. Her voice was samaritan silk.
Her eyes went to slits, bronze fennel.
Something hula-hooped in my belly.

She said, 'Foxgloves. Velvet.
Darkness. Alice, I want it.'
He has forbidden her the house.
He can't see her standing on our path,
full sun, without a shadow. I found
honey in her fingers like the blind.

Archie

The eggs and clam croquettes in cream I'd shipped for lunch
weren't sure what to do about it, if you'll pardon the argot.
It was nearly two. I was thinking of hitting up the Thruway
when I spotted our customer. NVMS. No Visible Means of Support.
Bonton for bum. I nosed the roadster nearly to a stop
beside him on 52nd Street. Slim Folz, a dick who hates
my epidermis, was couched there behind the *Gazette*.
I trotted the brain around for a survey of the situation,
and eased on going with the speedo down under 40.

When I'm on my way for a man, everything I touch,
like the steering-wheel, seems alive with blood going
through it. The sharp air glistened in my lungs.
I heard a noise overhead, oil of almond fizzing
in a saucer from the hood. The crackaloo
woke me up good. I vamoosed like one streak
of lightning stopping another. The stuff spidered out
over the floor. I got propped on my coccyx again
and carried on rolling, throttle wide open on the decorum.

Safeguards

She kept changing. Strong,
mottled, silent, ingesting
Meryl Streep in the Dingo
Baby trial, she was a chameleon

that mounted every rainbow
in spitting distance.
A re-agent, detecting
levels of foetal blood

that might or might not be rust
in the spray-pattern
under the dashboard,
couldn't have solved her.

She was a Quatermass meteor
offloaded in my yard.
I had a Lorenz reaction
as if I'd whiffed

chasuble oil down the loo.
Now she's gone I've set up
mobile statuettes. Six
bronze-alloy, poison-tip

longhorns protecting
the bare patch – where I've planned
a well-fertilised *verbena*.
You have to be careful.

Outing

Why I always asked for him,
how he became my favourite,
I don't remember. Boot-nosed, brown,
smelly, he'd come out as I waited

and ignore me. Flotsam round him
like lost lettuce. No one else
thought him special. Chaplain says
you can have important love

for someone unimportant,
there's a down side to everything
and that sets you free. I think
she's up the creek. It was the name:

from the heart of Congo,
largest something, marsupial maybe,
in the world. Capybara. Having seen him
I'd go back to the penitentiary OK.

Biographer

Of the orgies on Yam Island
at the time of the Dogstar setting
when cannibals came who developed
an insatiable appetite for Spam,
I will not speak. I set out then
in a collapsible canoe, to test
her recipe for jellyfish stings:
papaya mixed with late-night pee
from a six year old boy
who has just learnt to swim.

I shall be buried with my Gold Card
in my folded right hand. In case.

What We Did

It was the birthplace of sages.
If you learned something there
you didn't forget it. New arrivals
remembered what they'd forgotten –
but their voyage had to have been
a long one.

When we landed, greedy for bitumen,
sarsen, golden dodos, *wragg,*
we came on an ashwood piano,
ingrown with thorn-formica.
A little blonde, dreaming
of a ghostly alcoholic

who'd play, over and over,
a broken A minor chord perfectly
in grey wool fingerless gloves.
She was waiting for it, really,
staring at us dumb that way
from her driftwood keys,

like a child who doesn't know
why she wants her sadness
to be seen. Well? What would you
have done? It was a town
in the land of Rum.
Now under water.

Still Life with Bible

He painted rain till it slashed the canvas,
found a new way of calling wind to surface,
making space shout. Tree-roots wisped
their impossibly thin sand. The disabled sky
boiled in his eyes. Disfigurement was how he loved,
possessed by wheat-spears' black in yellow,
the scorched ghost-road bubbling
a keyhole view of roots in hell together.

If the sick sun came now it couldn't purge
the mad grappling sky. The deepsea night café.
This night's end might be the start
of a day's work under the railway bridge.
A double vanishing point. An ugly fork
with nothing to be said for it but the way
he sees the cleft of buying and selling
on Avenue Montmajour.

And under the table, forgotten,
the little *Isaiah* for when his father died:
one of his own candles down to its wick,
a family bible, imaginary, black,
open at *acquainted with grief.*

Mary's First

She wants to leave me.
To continue as a white newt.
Tan-spotted, crested.
A large one. Handsome,
as newts go.

Her last human request
is to be pushed,
new gills pulsating,
into the orchestra pit
but racing green pondwater

sloshes from compartments
in her empty pram.
This holds me up and I lose her
under the seat of someone
unendingly angry.

We spot the screen
with our panicky silhouette
and some precision instrument
makes itself known
in my head, asking

What will you do now,
with the rest of your life,
plus the first bit,
that ended like this
in lost amphibia?

Filling them up

She's good at being wonderful
for other people. Can't help seeing
shadows of dirt on her own pane
when the late sun spurts. Gently,

reaching for what's wanted, she talks
behind those heads greasing up
her Viennese antimacassars.
They go off lighter. She turns to TV

and disappears herself
as if the things she was weren't here.
When you're small, your body's you.
Shitting. Griping. Hurting. How you learn.

It's what you blame for failing
like the girl who thought her arms too long.
Are you big enough, small enough, here?
Is this surface all the others need?

Then lines on the face are passports
to past mischief. Here come
the white hairs and backaches.
You can't do what you want.

Writing this up, she sees
she'll never ski,
or cross the Gobi desert,
ride through Mongolia, sail to Samarkand,

punt the Amazon. Nuzzle camels
in a spell of stars.
Suddenly, all to herself she is
a casket she's afraid of.

What's incubating here?
Already this odd familiar
holds the slow-sphinx
sickle-embryo of ending,

which she's not known to analyse away.
When patients go, she flicks
the light dust, tidies foxed flowers.
The room must be immaculate, for them.

Break-Up

Like a bad dream
where pressure plummets
in the lion-scrub oil-wells,
the fibreglass mastodon
crooks up in its molten mud
at Fossil Beach,
the real-estate merchant
in his earthquake-proof
ninety-floor high-rise
sends his secretary home,

and on underground screens
mesmerising the only
slightly bent mayor
who plucked his family
out to Palo Alto,
a blue crackle of faults,
like a demonised Fizzing John
at Halloween, volleys up
the unthinkable. Nothing like
he'd been told.

II

Godfearing

We listened for the ringing of a bell,
catnapped between electric
muezzin calls. One of us

caught a photo of a mirage
on the asphalt over Ur,
the very spot, said someone,

where Abraham set out
into the Talmud, into the Qu'ran,
into the small

unbothered Saxon churches,
into the sixty-foot Bleeding Heart,
dripping eternal neon in Tennessee.

They've named a war for a racehorse,
sent us to the Assyrian desert
to interview

a pilot in chocolate chip uniform:
a brave boy, briefed
to avoid mosques and never gloat.

So how did he feel
making the first score,
when he turned another plane

into a comet-hair fireball?
A man like him, in there?
Who had a family, like him?

The difference, he guesses,
is the country he comes from.
On the right side. GODFEARING.

Where They Came From

Their own treasure, ironglass saints
and nativity, the blue spectaculars,
lay wrapped in the Colne-bed
centuries after the war, and now jet cobalt
through the honey-limestone church.
When sun shines. When anyone's there to see.

On the greengold hill behind,
plane-spotters watch for bombers.
'If you're going to make a carpet
you might as well make a big one'.

A frisson when B-52s appear
through foreign cloud. 'It's wonderful.'
'Like Christmas.' Pub and bank
are open through the day.
Both accept dollars. 'Fairford'
is emended 'Nuke Kuwait'.

Mesopotamia has no stone. They wrote
on river clay. If you go to Chicago
the great excavators will show you
Babylonians treasured imported stone

and if you travel over Iraq by air
you see cities all round. Every mound
of dirt is a city. In no place
can one stand and not see two, or three,
on the horizon. The question is not finding
a city but which one to choose.

Fairford: Cotswold town. Saved its church glass in the English Civil War
by burying it in the river. Also an air-base.

Guide to the Balawat Gates

This mound was the temple of Mamu,
god of dreams. Nimrud's desert nipple.
War archives, begun in a sandstorm
where Assurbanipal

buried clay bibles of cuneiform
under the floor, glazing
roof and gates with bronze so high
I'd have to take the six of you
on my shoulders to touch top.

Hinge-graphics, look,
embossed with cross-stitch swords
sliding home, give us the killing-rate
for Shalmaneser II's campaign

and here in the corner, the West Hinges
recorded in photos. My photos.
I'll show you – it took years –
how they have been restored,
sent back and set up in Iraq.

Bulletin

We saw film of fireworks like crosses
zoom on a blue building
and were told it was victory.

There were reports of water installations
surgically erased. We thought the city
would smash under children's feet.

We learned that talk was no good,
yet the ones who directed the guns
seemed to care, as if telling us lies

was important. No one went to the theatre.
We avoided large stations
and went home early,
depressed at the thought of news.

The Conqueror

He commanded a Letter to God.
My soldiers are valiant eagles.
They jumped the Zab
as if it were a ditch.

He ruled a country of rivers,
barley, fish, bilharzia.
There were spindle-whorls, maps,
interpreters of dreams,

Nissaba, goddess of schools,
bi-lingual syllabaries.
A core curriculum
fostered the literacy rate.

Consider the wonders of the cosmos
for there is also Namtar,
vizier of the underworld,
god of sixty diseases.

Rosa Silvestris Russica

John by Grace of God Botanist Royal,
from the British expedition
against Russia, 1618,

brings back a Russian vest.
'Stockens without heels'. Snow-boots
to walk on snow without sinking.

Soldiers die of frostbite, heartache,
diarrhoea, plague. He collates
'Things by me Observ'd',

falling most in love
with Russian roses. 'Wondros sweet'.
All the deck back

he keeps alive a Briar of Muscovy,
the ambuscad's one prize.
How else should a scientist work

but join the politicians'
raids on other worlds?
Afterwards he labours

in his South London garden
on the names of roses.
Little lights of the field.

Tudor Garden, Southampton

We are plotting a tunnel of tree poles
to rose-terraces and fishpond.
Our herb-hedge stars the names. Hyssop,
dwarf sage, properly in adjunct.
Enlarging shadows fold our home
in protection at All Hallows Eve.

The jagged lightning ash spoils things.
It nudges at endings. My father
tells a boy to shore it down.
I tend a knot of green rainbows.
Homegrowing emblems clinch us
to Court. To the Colonies. Each Spring

shouts out our trust in constellation.
We're part of things. We've heard
of voyages of ambush, new plants from abroad.
Rose-wine lips our stone jugs in the bower.
I clip and tie. My father takes drink
with the men who remain.

In the harbour you can almost see,
the greyed fleet slinks and nods.
I've seen it other years: the burnt boys
carried last, when everyone's gone.
My brother won't come. From this stone
you hear the flags snap on the wind.

My mother talks to plants, tells me
their names, not writ down,
and conserves medicine upon our hurts.
At night my father bends upon new maps,
while she traps fleas in tubes
of china clay, sewn in under my skirts.

Passing it on

Take Kevin. Laid off Ford. Came home
late from the Bird and Baby,
took an eight-and-a-half-inch

silver-plated corkscrew
from the box presented
on retirement to his dad,

Latin motto inscribed,
as was traditional, on its lid,
and hammered his Alsatian's

barking head
to the diamond-flash
vinyl-quilted floor.

Without

They decided they'd keep just the head.
I heard she was imposing
recession régime on the household
(three little boys

and they were asleep now
anyway, missing things),
because another body,
female, wouldn't do.

I shimmied in early but
the others had got there first
and in she came, all
buttoned-through Jaeger

for the occasion.
I couldn't speak for tears
but she wouldn't see me anyway.
She sailed up smiling,

reeling in the bouquets
like Thatcher after the war
on telly, at the little
top of her steps.

This way, you can have it sent.
It's a service, like any other.
No screams, no mess.
Because it's easier without.

You haven't to bother
over the mysteries and waste.
Nothing to get in the way.
But all I could think of

was a head in a box
arriving later from the hospital.
Mentally female, once female,
all future

in a thermo-nuclear vaccuum,
dreaming of bodies to hold.
Bodies she'd build for
herself, one day.

On the Ice Label

I got there through the battle-zone
leaving a four-year-old
alone with 6 oz puma paté
for the day. Someone had taken
another shot at the Booker winner,
a guy with an electronic voicebox
in a roller-chair. The cops were out.
Rocket-launchers on white vans
down the Strand. Fire in bottles.
Catshouts over health-cuts. Caltrops.
TV crews in khaki. You know the pitch.

We had string quartet that day
with the reggae. His *Dies Irae*
under the griffin-claws
of a de-sanctified cathedral
with a seven-minute decay
on the *re*verb – dead right
for serpent, ophiclide, bassoon.
That's the last I saw of him.
The two of us were double glazing,
two walls of mismatched dust,
glaring at each other. I've learned
the corner the light doesn't reach
is the one the dime rolled to.
But we cut that disc OK.

Forgetting *Rosemary's Baby*

The last decapitated belisha
on our island down Abbey Road,
can't get rid of its head,
still flashing on brown live wire.

In the Children's Zoo,
a wallaby blinded by a peacock
turns its sly white
eye-crack towards us.

In the national interest
four hundred cheap
Filipino deaf-mutes
tap international criminals

on laser file at the request
of ministers in a tax-free uniform,
peaches-'n'-gelignite Armani glasses,
whose Steering Committee

on the curbing of music in schools,
signs the Official Secrets Act
over four bottles of warm
white Portuguese wine.

Trees

(for Thomas, November 1989–February 1990)

> *In the centre grows the Plane Tree of Hippocrates, 45 foot in diameter, its branches propped on ancient marble fragments. Tradition says Hippocrates taught in its shade. The principal excursion is to the Sanctuary of Asclepius, two and a half miles by road.*
> GUIDEBOOK TO THE ISLAND OF COS

1

It's always sunrise here
as long as the generator lasts.
His eyes are a surprise. Dark
under his nylon wired-up hat.

The only vein they could get into
was his head, shaved three months
before he was due. He stares
over the oxygen-clamp on his nose

through a wall of plastic at his mother.
The scratched sides change sparkles
when walkers hurry and squeak
over the floor he knows nothing about.

There are other tense Snow White shrines
in this forest of technical piping,
a museum of people
who came too early or wrong.

The lookers have the most connected feel,
waiting in T-shirts, bulging, terribly hot.
The nurses dread each wizened arrival
(half don't stay) but do their best –

at Christmas a sterilised red sock,
distended with signed photograph
to mummy and sometimes daddy,
by the corner of each glass tray.

2

She lives in hope at the breast pump,
and on the road to the hospital.
For the first time she takes photos madly
with a new idiotproof camera. She hasn't held him.

The consultant says he still could go. She sits
putting back the air-tube when it falls.
He doesn't know he's waiting or what's waiting
for him. But once, once, he smiled.

3

Pink-brown of chafed gold,
salt-cellar hidden from soldiers
under the bee-hives,

time-piece of wrinkles
to be wound up gently by hand,
docketed on his cushioned shelf,

waiting for a sale, the right sale,
porcelain and amber machinery
ahead of its time,

temperature graph turning
bluely in the corner,
tense-eyed as a pup

in the wired-off back of a car
with the window up tight,
he gazes, often irate,

through scratches in cloudy plastic
at this outfit where the lick
of temple snakes flush with bacteria

might be the only deciding touch
you never know about
of god in the prayed-for,

incubated dream,
and here outside
gales rip three million trees

from earth bewitched
by fluorescence. Even a twig
would bust his wine-glass bed.

4

Over on the snake-god's island
the chimney-pot plane tree
drops another arm of its bulk,

slowly inviting antique jags
of marble to press closer in,
scarring its multiform self

to the heart, while saying anything
about him seems unfair:
someone so eager to be here

that they gave what was needed,
fast jets of oxygen
blasting the little lung.

Now they drain
the sores these make,
he is a miniature

hydraulic St Sebastian.
In his only body
steroids battle infection.

This is the chance
for tissue to build, if it will.
He lies and fights

for air
and his bruise-eyes wander
and he can't be hugged.

III

Crimson

The dye grew
as hairy *fettucini*
swags of moss
up a giant plum tree.

You had to go carefully
to gather it, for somewhere
in the khaki forest
where they harvested

our raw crop,
swarms of fierce
bees hung: the guardians.
This was never spelt out

but we knew. Plus,
on a marble shelf
in the Garden Room
beside the secateurs

and snipped ends,
lay a smashed-up
kitten in a box.
Almost invisible wounds

in its withers.
Upper eye corroded
like a rusty sequin
by one splash.

Trance

She was a sea anemone
with spittle on it.
A dark red eye
sucking at the physics
and geometry of knots

with lemons in the head
like cirrus beards of *Dairy Milk*
and, if you half-shut your eyes,
like purple eggs hanging wrong
in the apple tree at twilight.

His tongue in her teeth
was a young slug
rampaging on dandelions.
A contortionist playing Puck.
But all this was nothing much:

as if you'd lived a maimed
horizon, and your eyes,
accustomed to black
sappy woods, can't take
perspective on the plain.

Saturday Night at the Firehouse

She'd had that dream again, the one
where they cleared the engine out,
ordered up gypsies with drums and tabasi,
and someone looking for her in the crowd.
Couldn't talk, but she knew he was there.
In real, the rubbed cement floor

with its dancing wishbone jeans
was nothing like it should've been.
Gone with the Wind. War and Peace.
Songs like *Lili Marlene.*

It wasn't she was looking for a prince.
Anyway judging from the British
princes were off. She knew
the good times come only once
or twice, matches struck in a dark,
none special if you have too many.

It was just if there'd been someone
she secretly knew was secretly
pleased she was there. No one local.
She imagined a very loose-hipped Colombian,

Jaguar Sam, all Tequila Sunrises for her
like the girl in *Goldfinger.* Hands
everywhere slowly, like a relief map
of the Great Lakes. A human volcano
that'd think he was God,
and evening squeezing into a song.

Instead, here she was
standing round in a hot allergic face
while her mind was roaring
through some night warehouse

ahead of V2 torches, desperate to match
the sea-pattern in her hands
with fabric on twenty-foot stacks.
Those gypsies were belting out
Give me the Girl on bamboolas
and it sounded wrong

but all the same on the ridgey floor
where the engine oil
they were all so proud of had oozed
in a stain like Madagascar, she met him,

beaked like a doctor in the plague
who enters a house with a cross on it
(marked 'God have mercy') in a leather mask,
eye-slits blocked in with glass,
gauntlets reaching to elbows,
cowslip-root pouched next the skin:

a man filled with broken light
sifting inwards like sharp fur-flakes
in a kettle. And afterwards it wasn't
at all what she imagined. But it did.

Watching *Oklahoma* with the Light On

Somewhere in a burnt
strip of the mind
a wolf howls
into the central heating

for innocence
in all its emerald
and yellow rayon
and fake Mozartian song,

and a manic side-drummer
stops music in its tracks
in rage at the lack of explanation,
and somewhere down a green ride

where trees touch overhead
two singers have been walking
through the night, his fingers
precise on her waist

down a moss path
she'll dream of
all her life to come:
this sloping avenue

to a cave they never saw,
a May-dawn shivery
roof of green coin,
and everything he said and felt

unquestioned as those warm
drops spawned in a rising sun,
that wicker hush, and the green
melt slipping away.

Indian Red

'You must know ferrous oxide,
rusted horse-shoes (not that we have
many horses), is hard work.

Backbreaking, even in shade.
Dissolving, dipping, scraping;
boiling re-used iron

for the dye you carry off. Children pee on it
to make it fast. You must know I'm on fire
each time I think you're here.

I know you don't think much of me.
You took me casually
under the pecaha tree,

as an ancient right of way between our hills
whose rule was tigers in my mother's day.
Your *Country Kitchens Worktops*

ate the trees and did for tigers
and that's one danger gone. You've done so much.
You must know you're my smell of grass

down the loneliest path of childhood,
the rust-reek of nettles where the foetus bled away
behind your workhouse, those so many years ago.

Everyone's a shit sometimes, I hear you say
in English: well, what I regret
is handing on the cloth

that bound my stomach when I knew, thrilled
till I got sick. Soft hibiscus, dotted red
with elongated buds – to think I let it go.

You're still the iron in my days. You must know,
yet I know you won't, you've never learnt my words
except for *That's too much* and *cut it down*,

you're the outside marvel to my one idiot life.'
So wrote the village weaver to the buyer from abroad
who paid the scribe twice over to forget.

The Wish

All night she waited naked in her room
for the man playing poker downstairs
with fifty-one cards, casual as the cleric
who snips the wax cascades
from boulevards of six-foot
emerald-ribboned prayers: Poland,
Ireland, Tierra del Fuego
taking their turn to burn
in the plaza before the basilica.

Barefoot she listened
to a silence with the light on,
then went back and dressed for bed
like a station porter wheeling back
the empties, tipped by the nuns, the medicos,
the extensively kitted, wellmeaning families:
passionate assistants clumsy with the bumps
over the three thousand kilometre venture
to the SNCF arrival platform, Lourdes.

The Guide

On their way down,
down the secret
rockdrop to the desert,
he stopped and through a crack

she saw a city, goldfrost
under the night. Acre,
perhaps. A floating wick
on oil. He bent, kissed,

then bit her lower lip.
She knew she'd come here
for this. This boxed land,
cloisonnéed with razor-tape,

roadblocks, petrol-candles,
tombs, and 60 mph red stones.
Plus mosquitoes. *Culex
fasciatus* on the razzle.

This glint of a many-times-
broken city she couldn't get at.
This four-by-four hole
of black heat: Nazareth

to Nablus, a long way
pregnant on a donkey. This kiss
of anthrax and caramel.
This torn-up host.

Harvest Moon

When night-mist from the hedge
tangles Milky Way whiskers to branches
of the hundred-year-fat oak
where I pee for the last time
at four in the morning under the stars;

when apple-moths leave the codlings,
and the Dog Star has set
over macintoshed sheaves of late wheat
giving off brightness
nothing to do with us;

and the faded family velvet
finally tears and falls:
I'll come to you
as in the old days,
singing an almost winter song,

high notes like separate pins of flame
in a circus nobody came to.
I'll be reconstituted a heron
opening my raw
orange under-skin

printed with snow-crystals,
under blanched kimono feathers
and dance in the white-
as-rice-paper stage-mist
that designates

the approach of a ghost,
and you'll return,
a saffron demon undone by lust,
your wandering
visible as snail tracks

through a thousand years of fog
in search of a land laid waste,
and there'll be two grave male faces
either side of us –
the master puppeteers.

We'll swim from the dark,
two long-sleeved
resinous figurines
requiring three manipulators each,
playing a lovers' last meeting

on a frosty bridge outside town
and beside us,
heartrending leaves
of imported silver paper
sing out a flickery nostalgia

for bamboo heartland
no one here has seen.
And apprentices, mobile
Ku Klux Klan fur stones
in black dominoes

and secretly translucent slub hoods,
will be moving our legs.
For in Bunraku
it takes a lifetime
to perfect the lower limbs.

Before Breakfast

The sea was spilling in like torn muscle,
pockmarked thundery silk
cold-slabbing a question-mark
up over the causeway

and she was looking for him
having lain three hours
not moving after his slip-out.

Her thighs still pricklèd
and she found him in someone's stable
filling with sun:

one elbow
squashing pale hay
and his long tweed back

– she could have counted
stressed vertebrae –
coiled round a hare. Both rapt;

his tongue in its mouth.
He was nibbling the whiskers
along to their root.

Down the road
she found another, purring.
When she tiptoed back

the hall-stairs flickered
with a hush of servingmen
who stared as if
she ought to have known.

IV

Ariadne at the 'Tricycle'

We sit in black
icicle roots. The gods'
electric spaghetti.

Twin saxophonists
work white-forked hose
and thick-gilt codpieces
across a baize stage.

Each is a glacé astronàut,
a hunting stork, a new-
painted god of machine,

ignoring the girl on a sandbank
in laddered black tights,
boring the pants off
an unattached phone.

She wrings her hands. Angelus
we could've all done
in our time alone:

Dido, Echo, Butterfly
on a black stone beach,
hearts cut like teeth
on an improvised throne,

as each man for whom
they dropped their leaves
of self, leaves them.

After the Show

The last thing I remember
is a shell of dead ivory
like the furred surround

of family photos, left when I asked
for the palace to be empty,
so I could empty it of me.

A stone cup at the window
fills with rain. Ariadne
can't imagine the ocean

through his head. How tears
are aliens' antennae, and women
lighthouse-shards. Eel-snags

in a crackle-glaze sea.
After the show it's hard
to snap out. Hard to go

without blaming the ship
men make and call 'she'.
Frost and mist cling as I leave.

Runners and Risers

I

'Start with a rubber negative.
The mould. Divide the body
in sections you fit together
at the end. Swill wax
against the rubber's inner face.
When it hardens, peel the rubber off
and add wax tubes. These ones,
the runners – with cups on top
where we'll pour the metal in
(pure aluminium, for this bugger) –
and risers to let the trapped air out
as the hot stuff settles inside.

II

'Paint the wax with white ceramic slip.
When *this* hardens it can be warmed
and never change. But the wax melts
like a woman, leaving two things:
an outer mould, exact negative
replica of the beast, plus inner core,
so the final figure – get it? –
will be hollow. What you've got
is an albino haggis. A white tangle.
Tubes you wouldn't recognise as body.
Fire him in sand. When he's hard,
you pour the metal – cream on fire –
in the narrow gap between the mould
and core. When this is cool, lift off
the core and mould. They're brittle,
prise 'em gentle. Snowcrust off dogshit.
Cut and chuck runners and vents.

III

'This is where you fit the bits together.
The original had Roman joints. Spigot
and socket. We used Argon Arc,
fusing without oxidising. No more
of the cold dry weld. Plus this cunt
had steel up his bottom leg
for the weight of his risky pose.

IV

'Patinating. We swept Indian ink,
finished in lanolin, over the silvery.
Shadows on frost. A black pearl finish
so the fine print, muscle and bone,
can be read across the circus.'
So the caster said in the foundry

over the roaring sawdust, to the woman
he'd given kids never brought to term,
herpes, twenty years loss: his Christmas
visitor in her nowhere marriage. Explaining
the restoring of Eros, lost wax method,
one arm round his this-winter girl.

Comeback

He was circumspect. Casual.
Easy to disown the after-effect
of what you only say

if you're used to charming metal,
City Councillors, the hidden
faults of granite. He hit

a mock self-deprecating note,
as if you took a chisel to an opal.
Not wanting to damage it.

Just to check again you could,
if you liked, see its heart.
What did she think had changed?

Each time snakes erupt in her
she thinks of him. He's put all this
aside. He talked of loneliness,

of not seeing spring again. She trembled
at how much she didn't want
a world he wasn't in. But when she came

back through his sky of black grapes,
there was Autumn. Lacy as an elderflower.
Available. Nicking champagne.

Her immunity shone like a wheel.
This was the one he led into the night
to celebrate his veteran's return.

Afterwards he sent Eurydice
a photo of his dustbin.
Off-cuts of steel and empties

at his kitchen door. An artist
in pain, still tapping one stone's
underworld, anachronistic flaw.

Girl with Bare Shoulders

She hates this painting.
Owes the model money.
Master takes this very girl
instead for the Muse, these days.

Her own body's over-thin
for sitting now. When he wants it
she gets dated notes.

'The master says to let her in
today.' The concièrge interrupts
through a curtain. Rodin says he's old.
He gets a headache afterwards.

Too much is bad for work.
She can't afford a fire.
Those coddled-egg-white eyelids

dip down at her cold floor.
*Stop seeing him! If you knew
how I burn! No one
who hasn't known it can –*

*you'll be the first
since me.* Her mongoose brush
juggles where his fingers

must have crisped their way
between those lard-cake thighs.
She labours through the chin
and beaking mouth before it opens

down the stairs. Laughing
through Paris streets.
All the cold way to him.

Mrs Dowland

Each time I see him I remember how it is.
That the contract's in my soul
not his. And – not quite true – as long
as he an't alone, that anyone'd do:

as though I'd agreed he wasn't bound.
And yet there's bondage somewhere.
Do I only imagine when he is alone,
feeling his body working on him older,

it's me he mostly minds about,
as he sends those songs
to some patroness of a thousand wigs
with maids to pearl her?

He says they bare his soul.
He writes from the court of a foreign prince
to laughing blondes with oak forests
and stone mastiffs,

who know how to live where they are.
I know him otherwise.
His yearning to impress –
one thing of many I can't say

I can't stand. Seeing him bounce
at courtliness that don't quite work,
and slump when we go back
to Fetter Lane: it makes me sick.

I see the women wonder
what he's like in bed. Some, I guess,
find out. I get the worries:
teeth, eyes, sore toe, debts.

He charms in Elsinore. I shut the door
and work for the Queen of Spades.
I run to other timetables, not his.
He makes me angrier than anyone,

disappears for years when he's happy
and ever more Danish girls-in-waiting
move his way along the battlements.
But his thickened cheeks blue in winter,

the famous lake clogs with leaves,
and when there's no one
he's spoken to for years
except to have a row or fall asleep,

I think I feel him think of me
across the sea. Half of me
wants a world he can't get into,
the other half despairs

that no one else I ever see
will do. *Upon my soul*
I understand it not,
he writes. But not to me.

On the Venom Farm

1

'My next bite is my last.'
Nine times bitten, Dennis
lifts the lid. Picks out
a Siamese cobra. 'Once bitten
I stay calm. I freeze my mind.
Walk off before it strikes again.
Phone friends. Don was the best
before a mamba got him. Snakes
or scotch. With all of us a toss-up
which gets us first.

'It's never the same. The snake
decides the dose. The last one,
now, the diamondback –
there was a terrible burning.
My vision crazed, like ice.
In thirty minutes I was paralysed.
Sicking up blood. Convulsed.
They 'coptered me to Portsmouth,
ticketed *Dead on Arrival*. My heart
stopped. Can't do that again.

I'm allergic to the serum, see.
I send World Health our milk.
Anti-venom's no more use.
I lost a lot of flesh.'

2

He loves them. When they're ill
he holds them, no gloves,
for the vet. In summer
he climbs into a pit of six

so tourists can see them angry.
We watch smoky knots uncoil.
Hands bare, squeezing the throat-gland,
whipping the tail where he wants it,

he milks the thing into a glass.
'After the snakes, I'm randy.
I tell women they've seen nothing like
a man with cobra in his blood.

A cricket box, though, is essential.'
He flicks the echoing mound
under his trousers. His redhaired wife
serves Margaritas rimmed with salt.

Heirloom

God of fungus no one noticed,
of relationships that haven't failed
but calcified so there's nothing to say

and not much to joke about,
she's the no-colour sky that isn't there
except for the planes

who must go on trying to fly through it.
Double X of the well-meant cream cleanser
whitening basins, poisoning the mud,

DNA of the thought that nothing will do,
even shopping or moving house,
she's bland and exacting,

her shrines are everywhere,
not humdrum but chasm places,
yet when you get out

they look like a fuss about nothing.
Her rites are the twisted bumper
and the nasal frightened rhetoric

of arguing who'll pay.
She rises from babycare,
blocked drains and woodlice,

taking us in: Queen of damp air,
darkness, and stalemate,
of watching your child

be the unkind one
who picks up the excluding cry.
Accidie's fellow-traveller,

lady of the row that didn't happen,
of malice repeated by someone who
halfway shares it, she laughs

from the mould of sliced bread
at soap opera, her cult-brochure.
The shell of her man-made smile.

Mistress of crossroads and cramps,
of half-alive, half-alone hours,
the home-woven, invisible

self of the shopping-arcade,
she lurks in the spasm
between saying you'll have coffee

and plugging the kettle in,
and when you look round for the others
she's the god of nothing else.

Dismembering the Minotaur

FRAGMENT 1: *Louvre*
With a bandaged finger
she rocks him on her knee,
a secret ex-innocent
and mooncalf with spotted skin

closed in by a key-frieze,
a zig-zag of young black ice.
Beside her, a three-legged basket
floats on a wall that isn't there.

FRAGMENT 2: *Berlin*
In his sanctuary,
dancing alone at the bottom of the cup,

busy with his own significance
under the blue chess game,

he is a sacrifice to himself.
A thing that needs to be killed.

He waits for the adolescent's
entry and quick exit, like a house.

A harp hangs in black air.
There is a stump of single tree.

FRAGMENT 3: *Brit. Mus.*
On the last cup, his death,
thumb up in a failed supplication,
his mad body tipping 45° erect,

a wavering missile
leaving the aircraft-carrier's deck.
But frozen: an appalled child

stepping for the first time
into sea. Like a man afraid
to put his arms round his wife.

V

Tonsils

When I had them out
I was promised
no more sore throats.
Ice cream every day
in hospital. A pack
of wild animal cards.

Afterwards I got taken
to the Humming-Bird House
at the zoo. *Have you Topaza Pella?*
No. *Heliothrix Aurita?*
No, I'm sorry. No.

I saw an anarchy
of little sleeves of flame
singe the wind
when we opened the door.

Harley Street

She was born round the corner
in an attic. Balancing
chemistry textbooks on her feet,
her father pushed the ivory
five-foot pram down the middle.

'He thought you were immortal'
says her mother. Later
she daggered sticks along
immaculate black railings.

But this day it's a psalm.
Every brass doorbell,
each blue-rinsed concièrge,
bland against the rush
of daily last hopes.

What's breeding behind the eye-slits
of the veiled chess Queen
whose biblical dress
feathers York paving

and Cornish granite
up the steps of Forty-Four?
Who have the sandblasted angels
on the cross with Queen Anne Street,
seen bereft today?

The worst are those waiting for a name
to something at work in a child,
pictured within
like leeches,

the sooty *tagliatelle*
in jars on the hospital shelf,
which the Middlesex
taught her father to apply
just under the eye-socket for a bruise.

Divination by Mirror

It was her job to look in the pool.
When she was little
meteors were stone stars
and balance was what fell.

As she, after due preparation,
leaning down to whorls of sacred oil
on the surface, till vapours
tickled her nose-hair,

might drop lost balance in
to the V-shaped sky.
Older, she understood
she mustn't draw conclusions

from what she saw in water,
whatever the number
of naked boys with spears,
nor conclude anything

from the precinct or sparky mountain,
though precinct was all she knew –
trained to decipher undertow,
and leave the implication to authorities.

There have to be some,
though they haven't turned up yet.
Not here, so out-of-the-way,
five hours from the nearest bar.

She fancied they'd be recognisable,
though not introduced. But anyway
what standards had she?
The temple opened

only the second day of each spring month
and her father's scrolls
spelt confinement. This thing of not
going on to test all.

Plus the goddess's armed withdrawal.
The temple was OK but hard to see,
except with braziers,
or where rosy roof-bricks

let in stripes of sun.
Her intimates were statues
foxed with smoke of burning innards.
Each month she oiled their worm-holes.

What was strange
was when she looked at night.
Perhaps it was that few inquirers came
– earth-oracles were two a kopek

in those days – but especially not at night,
so the basin was just for her.
Even when primrose sky
reared dark clouds

like blaming priests behind her,
the looking could be pale
as if it saw another night:
not like day but a chickenshell glisten

as Northern Lights in travelogues
might be if you saw them inside out,
peeling away the tissue
that stopped you getting there.

Seven with a Cross

The house boiled with panic,
with children who didn't talk,
brittly insincere. She found
she could say heartbreaking things
deadpan so no one would notice.

Pretending not to know was exhausting
and not really knowing
what she pretended not to know
was worse. She grew superstitious
which was at least private.

When pain presented itself
she wouldn't think of hopeful things
in case she unmade them.
She wrote seven with a cross
as if she were French.

On the Motorway

She comes a long way to meet me
but not far enough. Her hope
is flame in black bone,
gold warts under the skin,

a cassette of the Spring
Sonata played over and over.
Sixty-miles-worth.

The tigers in her dream
weren't angry. They were
just being tigers. I told her
if they hadn't been next door,

so visible over the fence,
they'd have been fine.
But next door had them both,

like one of those mirrory
embroidered Tamil
wraprounds, at the dustbin.
All kohl eyes and flashing apricot.

While her garden had none.
She tells me nights are the worst.
Sleeping-pills not-quite-working.

A lit strip under the door.
Dehydration. Guilt. Hypnopompic
flickerings of stacked-up balconies.
A stripe of narrow bed.

Magpies on the verge
dismember a fledgling.
Tail-lights embrace on the hill.

House of Night

She saw she was the one
in charge of the garden.

Bare earth
where there had been
cordon-apples. Cucumber frames.
Red gooseberries. Acanthus.

She tried explaining
to a man who takes away
dead trees (he must be me),

levering a heavy door
or Jacobean oak-board to his truck.

She stood on the back and helped.
The bolts had a guilty touch
of something solid flaking.
She said, but his job was clearance

and he didn't care,
'Just here were emperor lilies,
a chessboard of tree-peonies,

chocolate-and-copper
Romanian giant daisies.'

Surely she must have loved it.
The potting-shed, for instance,
had a tarry smell. Secret.
Exactly what was needed.

Seedlings bubbling in a mothy light
from patchy unwashed glass.
She was never enough there.

In the dream, her job's looking
for one bunch behind the walls

but all she finds
is autumn crocus clobbered by slugs.
It had a lonely taste,
and looks it now:

a wasteland reel of stumps.
So much, and she couldn't keep it.
This must have been her fault,

even so long ago.
Here's somebody whitening,

dying, maybe,
and a dim lost horse.
The man's gone with his lorry.
As I said, he must be me.

Good Night

When she gets back
the child hugs her neck
as if he'd never let go.

'Poor you,' says the mother,
'having all that to face
after a difficult day.'

Afterwards, alone with the glass,
she'll half-wonder,
was that where her love went:

footsteps down stairs,
a light you can't get more of
in an empty door,

a tug at a moving
face in the dark
shaking free hot rapt arms?

Peach Tree

Now that I'm going to leave you.
Now that I'm finally going
to put you on the market –

why do I see things carefully
only when I'm off? Leaf curl.
A headache. A wonder. Forty

white peaches rosy every day,
breaking like popped blisters
on the mad paths

paved by the sibyl of endless jigsaws,
who piled her thousand-piece
Old Masters in the shed. How can I leave

a free-standing peach tree,
my greenfrosted waste-mould
salad of broken-glass light?

Eclipse

Why does she feel everything she does
is illicit? Why is she always present
but not active at disaster,

like a journalist writing
for a paper no one reads?
Why does she see rupture all round her,

a terrorist whose handcuffs aren't paid for?
Why does she pay for them herself?
What is that night-time road of hers,

shallow black from a bus-stop
seen from a corner of the eye,
a reminder, never quite lit,

that home is lonelier
than walking to it?
When I try to help she shies off

at the most dangerous thing.
Yet this is why she comes. Afterwards
I stand at the other window.

The one only I use. I wriggle
the curtain back to free the moon
whose eclipse fits so accurate

in my sights. I leave it
to reflect itself. A bitten fist.
An *alter ego* in my leather chair.

To Boaz

You're the only one I don't invent.
Who still seems to surprise. Must be
remote control, a trick of the jacklight.

Anything my side our green line
is mirrors, gunbarrel-smooth.
You say, 'You can't have everything.'

Over there in the West, in desert
garyads, you're out of bounds
among the tall, bitter papyrus.